How to Build a Robot

How to
Build a Robot

by Steven Lindblom

Thomas Y. Crowell   New York

Photo credits: Musee d'Art et d'Histoire, Neuchâtel, Switzerland, page 6, 7; Museum of Modern Art, New York, page 16; 20th Century-Fox, page 32; MGM, page 33; Lucasfilm Ltd., 1977, page 42, 43; Cincinnati Milacron, page 57; Heath, page 67.

Library of Congress Cataloging in Publication Data
Lindblom, Steven.
    How to build a robot.

    Summary: Discusses the nature and history of robots
and the technological requirements for making them move,
sense, and "think."
    1. Robotics—Juvenile literature. 2. Robots—
Juvenile literature. [1. Robots. 2. Robotics]
I. Title.
TJ211.2.L558 1985   629.8′92   84-45336
ISBN 0-690-04441-0
ISBN 0-690-04442-9 (lib. bdg.)

To Benjamin and Nicholas Friedman —————————————

Contents

_1 / What Is a Robot?

Will robots take over the world? They already have! All over the world robots are quietly at work, doing all kinds of jobs quickly and efficiently.

But just what exactly is a robot, anyway? Is it any mechanical person, no matter how stupid or clumsy it might be? Or any smart machine that can make decisions for itself as it goes about its job? Or is it an intelligent, humanlike machine, with arms and legs and a head, that can move and think like you and me?

Science fiction fans will hold out for the last definition, and in a sense they'll be right. Whatever the robot has become since, it was originally the invention of science fiction. The word *robot* itself comes from a Czech word for forced labor or drudgery. It was made up for a futuristic play in 1920 by Karel Čapek, a Czech writer. His robots (which were actually androids) ran amok, as science fiction robots have ever since. The word, though, tells us something about what we hope robots will someday be: machines that will free people from drudgery. And robots are doing just that, but they are the other kind of robots, the smart machines, which don't look or act at all human but look like, well, *machines*.

While there are thousands upon thousands of "thinking" machines hard at work, in factories and even in outer space, the only humanlike ones have been those built for movies, publicity stunts, or even just for fun. And almost to the last one they are what robot fans call show robots, or *show-bots*, because they can't do much by themselves. They either are radio controlled, have a person inside operating them, or are capable of doing only a few simple tricks.

Čapek may have given robots their name, but he didn't invent the idea. All through history man has been intrigued by the thought of bringing to life an obedient replica of himself. Myth and legend are full of accounts of early artificial humans: Golems made of clay and brought to life by magic; walking statues; and homunculi, living creatures made by alchemy.

Greek myths tell how the god Hephaestus was supposed to have built several mechanical people, including two beautiful women of gold who followed him around, and a fierce mechanical warrior. Daedalus, who was an early engineer, was said to have built two walking statues that guarded the labyrinth on Crete where the half-man, half-bull Minotaur was kept.

It's hard to separate myth from reality in these tales, but we do know that moving statues of gods and animals, powered by water or hidden persons, were kept in temples

The Robot and Its Cousins

Android ■ An artificial person grown or built from flesh instead of mechanical parts, or any robot that looks like a person rather than a machine. So far only found in sci-fi (we hope!).

Automaton ■ A giant windup toy. A mechanical person (or animal) run by clockworks or motors, but able to do only repetitive, automatic actions.

Cyborg ■ In sci-fi, a half-man, half-machine combination, usually a robot with a human brain.

Golem ■ A huge, powerful clay man brought to life with magic spells. From medieval Jewish folklore.

Humanoid ■ Human-appearing robot (or alien!), or an android.

Industrial robot ■ A machine that can run itself, as used in modern factories. Often consists of a computer-controlled arm mounted on a pedestal base.

Mechanical man ■ A modern automaton. Not too long ago a robot and a mechanical man were one and the same. Now we use this term to distinguish a showbot from a real, "smart" robot.

Robot ■ In science fiction, a "smart" mechanical man. Now used to mean any "smart" machine; the combination of a computer and a machine.

Showbot ■ A show robot, built for looks but with little or no "brain," and usually either remote controlled or able to do only a few simple tricks. Usually seen at amusement parks, shopping malls, and on TV.

to awe worshippers. Most people in those days would never have seen any machine more complicated than the wheel, and would have been easy to impress. Daedalus's guards could have been little more than ordinary statues, perhaps with a swinging arm or two, gliding along on wheels or tracks.

As man's mechanical skills improved, so did the mechanical people he made. The Chinese, as early as the fourth century, built elaborate mechanical people and animals, among them a Buddhist monk that would beg for alms.

The West lagged behind the East, but by the thirteenth century European clockmakers and inventors were busily making clockwork "robots" too, which could play musical instruments, write, and draw. A few were actually destroyed by people who thought them the work of the devil, so realistic did they seem.

Most of these were what we call automatons, because they were able to do automatically only the one or two things they were built to do. Usually, but not always, they were run by clockwork gears and springs inside.

One, a chess-playing Turk built in Germany in 1769, worked so uncannily that it's never been explained how. It's fairly certain, though, that there was a person hidden inside, who would move about to avoid being seen as doors were opened to allow people to inspect the insides.

Another automaton, a knight in armor, was built in England in 1870. Run by a steam engine, it would strut along blowing smoke from a cigar in its mouth!

Robot fever really hit between the two world wars when the world went machine crazy. With taller buildings, bigger and faster planes, and ocean liners pushing back the limits of what was considered possible, there seemed no limit to what technology could do. All over the world backyard inventors, inspired by Čapek's play and the science fiction

Automata

Maybe they weren't really robots, but the automatons of the late 1700's and early 1800's were the next best thing, and, for their times, brilliant pieces of craftsmanship and mechanical ingenuity. And they were able to do far more than you would ever suspect a clockwork mechanism could do.

A Japanese inventor, around the year 1800, built an automaton to fetch sake from the neighborhood wine shop. His automaton, a large doll, would make its way through the streets to the shop, turning at all the right corners, and wait until the flask it was carrying was filled before it would return home. Since the mechanism to start it home was triggered by the weight of the flask, it could not be cheated; it wouldn't leave until the flask was filled to the brim.

The automaton in the picture was built in Switzerland in 1773. The boy writes on a piece of paper with a quill pen. Each letter is properly formed according to the rules of good penmanship, and the automaton's eyes move to follow the pen across the page. This automaton survives today in a museum in Neuchâtel, Switzerland.

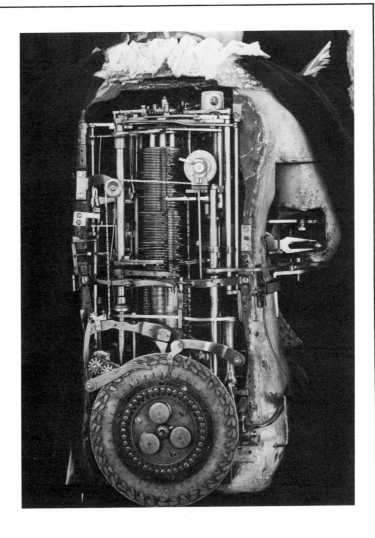

A look at the mechanisms will convince you that, whatever else these automatons were, they were neither primitive nor crude. Beside them the hydraulics and electrics of a modern robot look messy and obvious.

1930's Mechanical Man

and mechanics magazines of the day, were bolting together mechanical men. But instead of clockwork they used electric power and the newest of science's marvels, the radio, which let their creations be controlled from a distance, the way radio-controlled model airplanes are today.

All these machines, however much they astonished the people who saw them, had one flaw in common with the showbots of our time that kept them from being considered true robots. They couldn't "think." The automatons were really no more than incredibly complicated windup toys, able to do just one thing over and over again. Without "brains" they were, as you might expect, not very smart. Take the pen and paper away from the drawing automaton and it would go on drawing in the empty air.

8

Today we'd consider an automaton a *fixed-sequence* robot, because it follows a preset program that tells it what
to do. Many automatic machines in factories work this way.
Fixed-sequence machines can fool you into thinking they're
a lot smarter than they are, because they can do very complicated and precise jobs without anyone to run them. But
they aren't really any smarter than a music box because,
just as the music box cannot decide to change its tune,
the fixed-sequence machine cannot change its program.
The same machine that would look very clever drilling
and shaping a piece of metal would look pretty stupid doing
the same thing to a lump of ice cream. But it wouldn't
know the difference!

Actually, the dividing line between fixed-sequence and
real robots is hard to draw. Even the smartest robot usually
uses some fixed-sequence programs. And so do we when
we do things, like walking or throwing a ball, which we've
done so many times that we do them without thinking.

But what about the mechanical men, the remote-controlled ones? The trouble with them is that someone always
has to be at their controls directing every move they make.
That doesn't make sense if the robot is supposed to be
doing tedious work to free people for something more interesting, especially since the mechanical men are so
clumsy, it usually would be easier for their operators to
do the job themselves.

That's not to say such a machine doesn't have its uses.
It could work in places its operator couldn't safely go or
do things the operator wasn't strong enough to do. But

that's the job of a tool, not a robot, and that's all such mechanical men are: tools, no matter how fine they may look.

A true robot, most robotic experts today would agree, must be able to "think," move, and sense. Without these three elements, a machine can't be a robot. A radio-controlled mechanical man is really only a puppet, since it can't make a move without someone pulling on its radio-beam strings. An automaton, or any other fixed-sequence automatic machine for that matter, doesn't "think" any more than the mechanical man does. It doesn't need someone to tell it every move, but it can't change its program to handle the unexpected.

A truly smart machine like a robot must be able to carry out complicated instructions in spite of changes or the unexpected. Remember the automaton drawing in the air? A true robot in the same situation would find itself another pen and paper or stop trying to draw until it had them!

It wasn't until recently that it became possible to make a true robot. What made robots come true was the perfection of small, powerful computers that made it possible to give robots their brains and the power to think.

Is a computer a robot? Computers are often called "thinking machines," but that's not quite the same thing as a smart machine. That's where the second of a robot's essential elements, movement, comes in. A computer isn't a robot because it can't act for itself, since it does not have the power of movement. So, just as a mechanical man is not a robot because it can move but not think, a computer

is not a robot because the computer can think but not move. But put them together and you've really got something. Almost, that is.

That leaves senses. You might not think a robot would need to feel, but without senses there can be no thought. We've said that a smart machine will be able to handle changes in its program and, to a limited extent, the unexpected. But without senses, how is it to know when a change occurs? The drawing automaton would go on drawing with the paper removed. Why not? It has no way of knowing if the paper is there or not. It makes no sense to tell a robot, for example, to stop plowing at the end of a field, if it has no way of knowing when it reaches the end of the field. Or to go on grinding a lump of metal until it's smooth, if the robot can't feel whether it is smooth.

Fortunately for us, giving a robot senses is easy. The necessary hardware has been around for a long time. The

11

catch always was that without a suitable brain, there was no way for a robot to make use of the information senses could provide. But the computer has changed all that.

If we finally have all the technology available, then why hasn't anyone built a "real" robot yet, one that looks (at least a little), moves, and thinks like a human? Why have all the really fine-looking robots been fakes? There's a number of reasons. The best way to understand them is to pretend to be cybernetic engineers and build one ourselves, even if it's only on paper. In doing so we'll learn about the technologies a robot builder can use, and the choices that must be made: the alternatives the designer must consider and how these shape the robots that are actually built.

To make it a little simpler, we'll start with an arm, because this is the most difficult to build and the most essential part of the complete robot. Building it will draw on all the technologies that will be needed to build the entire robot. Since we've seen that to be a robot, a machine must be capable of motion, sense, and thought, we can break down the robot into those systems and handle them one at a time.

_ 2/ Motion _____

Our own human arms are made up of muscles and bones. The muscles do the work, but the bones provide the structure to support the muscles and give the leverage muscles need so that they can do their work.

Our robot arm will need mechanical parts to take the place of our muscles and bones. It will need motors or some kind of power to make it move, and a skeleton on which we can hang these power units and all the other parts the robot arm will need.

This skeleton must be strong enough to support the loads the robot may be lifting, and must have hinged joints that will bend in the right places, as our arms do.

We can build this skeleton either of two ways. It can be an external one, or exoskeleton, like a lobster shell or suit of armor, or it can be an internal one like our own. The choice will depend on what we are designing the robot to do. If we need a robot to mine on the moon or tame savage wolves, a chrome steel exoskeleton would be just

Interior skeleton
meets
Exterior skeleton

the ticket. Like the suit of armor, it would enclose and protect the working parts inside.

An internal skeleton, on the other hand, would be simpler and faster to build. It would also be easier to work on, since all the other parts the robot will need will be out in the open and easy to reach. This is especially useful for an experimental robot, since we can quickly make changes and adjustments. Making repairs on a robot with an exoskeleton might be a job for a safecracker.

Our robot will use an internal skeleton. We can always cover the machinery with an outer skin: metal, for a traditional robot look, or even a soft skinlike plastic if we're building the robot to baby-sit or give backrubs.

15

The False Maria Robot from *Metropolis*

Fritz Lang was the George Lucas of 1930's Germany. He made thrillers and sci-fi movies, one of which was so well researched that when the Nazis came to power, they confiscated all the copies they could lay their hands on so it wouldn't give away German rocket secrets!

Metropolis is about a city of the future, where airplanes fly up and down the streets between huge skyscrapers. But tucked away in a corner of this ultramodern city is as mad a scientist as you'll ever find. He creates a robot to take the place of a girl, Maria. The robot is probably the finest ever seen on the screen. Unfortunately, early in the film some scientific hocus-pocus transforms the robot into an exact replica of the girl, and for the rest of the film they are both played by the same actress. The robot reappears only briefly as a mob burns the false Maria, and the skin peels away to show the scornful and fireproof face of the robot beneath.

This fine old film has just been rereleased, with a new rock music sound track.

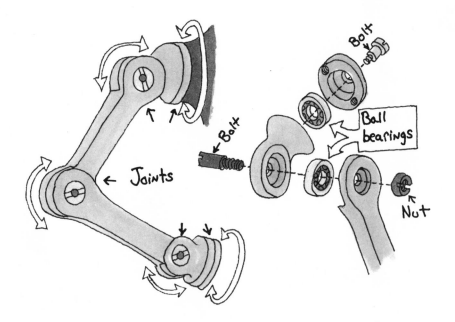

The skeleton framework itself will be metal. Aluminum is a good choice because it's light, strong, and easy to work with. The skeleton will need joints that can bend like the joints in our own arms. For joints that have to move in only one direction, like the elbow, we'll use ball bearings, like the ones in a roller-skate wheel, so the joint will move easily and smoothly. For other joints, like the wrist, which must be able to move in several directions, we will need two separate sets of ball bearings, one to handle the movement in each direction.

A skeleton isn't much use without muscles. Our robot will need some sort of power system to make it move. Electric motors are an obvious choice, but there are a couple of problems with them. One is that they produce rotary motion—that is, they produce power by spinning a shaft. Our muscles, on the other hand, produce power by pulling in a straight line. Engineers call that linear motion, and we'll need the same kind of movement from our robot's muscles if it is to move like a human. That means that if we use electric motors we'll have to find a way to convert their rotary motion into linear.

The other problem is that, in order to put out much power, electric motors must either be very big or spin very fast. Since no one wants to use a bigger and heavier motor than they have to, most electric motors are designed to turn at least several thousand revolutions a minute. While that may be fine for spinning a fan or powering a saw, it's too fast for powering our robot's arm, so we'll

LINEAR TO ROTARY + BACK

The Screw

The Crank

The Pulley

There are a lot of ways to convert linear to rotary motion, and back. This machine uses four of the most common.

The Rack and Pinion

need a way to slow the motor down without losing power.

Both these problems are familiar ones, and were solved hundreds of years ago when people first started building machines. The crank is the most common way of converting rotary motion to linear, but gears, screws, and other devices can do the job as well. Fast-turning motors can be geared down, without losing power, by using belts and pulleys, chains and sprockets, or gears.

You can see both these principles hard at work when you ride your bicycle. Your legs push the pedals up and down, which is linear motion. The crank arm converts that into rotary motion and turns the chainwheel. But the rear wheel has to move faster than your legs, if you're going to go anywhere faster than you could walking or running, so the chain and sprockets step up the revolutions to the back wheel. It, in turn, converts rotary motion back into linear as it pushes you and the bike along the road.

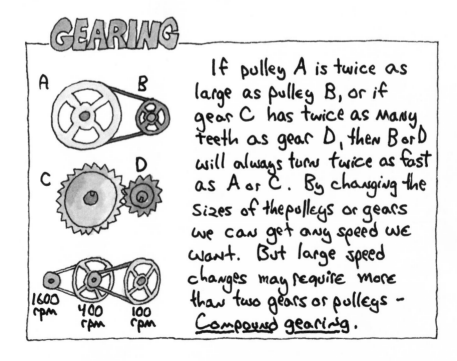

GEARING

If pulley A is twice as large as pulley B, or if gear C has twice as many teeth as gear D, then B or D will always turn twice as fast as A or C. By changing the sizes of the pulleys or gears we can get any speed we want. But large speed changes may require more than two gears or pulleys – <u>Compound</u> gearing.

A B

C D

1600 rpm 400 rpm 100 rpm

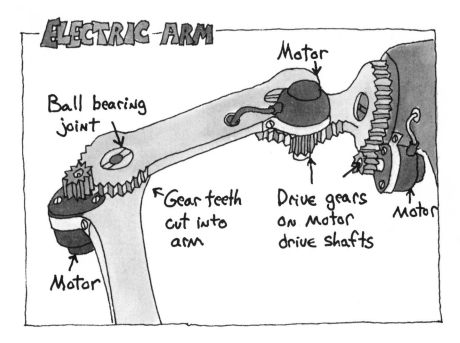

ELECTRIC ARM

Motor

Ball bearing joint

Gear teeth cut into arm

Drive gears on motor drive shafts

Motor

Motor

Of all these choices, gears would probably be the best since they take up the least space. But all these systems are complicated, so in deciding which to use we must remember the golden rule of engineering—K.I.S.S.—*K*eep *I*t *S*imple, *S*tupid! That is to say, do the job in the simplest way possible.

This may seem like a lot of trouble to go through in order to use electric motors, but they have their advantages, too. The biggest is that once they're hooked up, only two little wires are necessary to power and control them. And the motors, and all the gears to go with them, are cheap and easy to find ready-made.

If we decided to use electric motors, we could mount them directly on one side of each joint in the robot's skeleton. A tiny gear on the motor's drive shaft could drive teeth cut into the other side of the joint, making a very neat and compact set-up. When the motor turns, the little gear on its shaft moves the gear teeth cut on the arm, making the arm move. Whatever gears we'd need to slow down the motor could be built right into the motor housing. Motors like this are called *gear reduction motors.*

There's another kind of electric motor especially suitable for robot use, the *stepper motor.* As the name implies, instead of spinning around, these move in tiny steps of a degree or so each time the electricity to them is switched on. This makes it easy for them to make very tiny precise moves.

By keeping careful count of the number of jolts of electricity the motor gets, and how many "clicks" it moves in each direction, it can be made to repeat complicated moves exactly, which is very useful in a robot.

Another good possibility for powering our robot arm is a hydraulic system. Hydraulics use a powerful pump to force oil through hoses to wherever the work is to be done. The oil is under very high pressure: one to two thousand pounds per square inch, or about thirty times what a good bike tire will hold. Usually the oil is used to push the piston and rod in a hydraulic cylinder back or forth, although it can be used to turn a motor.

Between the pump and the cylinder is a control valve that lets us control how far and in which direction the piston will move. In a robot this valve would be operated electrically by the robot's brain. One pump can run many cylinders, but each cylinder will need its own control valve.

HYDRAULICS

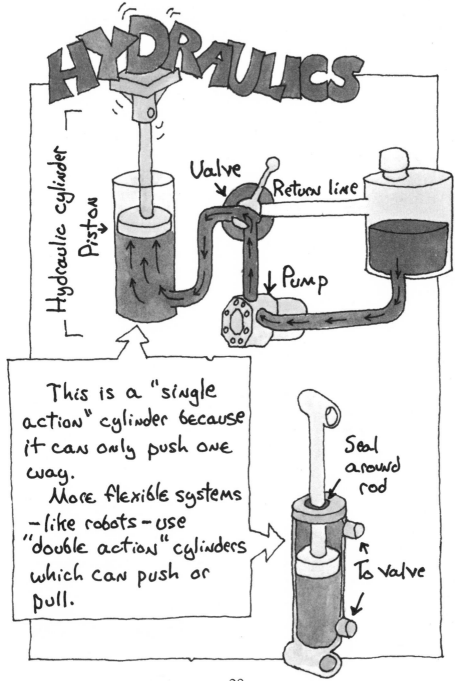

Hydraulic cylinder

Piston

Valve

Return line

Pump

This is a "single action" cylinder because it can only push one way.

More flexible systems — like robots — use "double action" cylinders which can push or pull.

Seal around rod

To valve

The oil in a hydraulic system, incidentally, isn't burned or used up. It's only a means of transmitting the power, as the chain on a bicycle is. Oil is used instead of water or some other fluid because oil won't easily boil or freeze, and also keeps the pump and cylinders well lubricated so they won't wear out. Air could be used, but an air system is "squishy" and not as precise. That's because air will compress under pressure, taking up less space, which a liquid like oil won't do.

Hydraulic systems are used on all sorts of farm and earth-moving machinery, as well as for steering and other controls on airplanes and trucks. In fact, if you want to see what a large robot's arm might look like with hydraulic power, take a look at the next backhoe you see.

Hydraulic cylinders used to be just about the best thing going for a large robot's muscles because they push and pull like our own muscles do, and with great strength and precision. Since they move relatively slowly compared to the fast spinning of an electric motor, they require no gearing and can be mounted on the robot's skeleton, just like our own muscles are on skeletons.

But hydraulic systems leak oil as they get old, and use cumbersome hoses and valves instead of wires and switches, and new high-tech electric motors designed especially for robotic use have eliminated most of the disadvantages of electric motors. As a result, most new state-of-the-art industrial robots use electric motors.

Whatever the system used, the biggest problem will be fitting it all in. Every motor will need at least two wires, plus whatever gears or pulleys it needs to work. Every cylinder will need two hoses.

If necessary, we can always simplify, especially in the hand. If the robot must be able to play an electric guitar or type, it'll need full control of each finger. But if it just needs to be able to rip autos apart or crush buildings, we can fix it so all four fingers operate together off one motor or cylinder and the thumb off another. Then we'll need only two cylinders instead of sixteen. Or we can combine the four fingers into one pincer, like a lobster's claw.

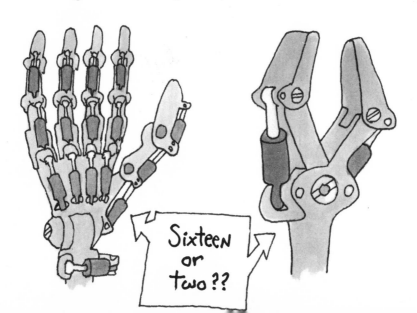

Sixteen
or
two??

Which system should we use for our robot? Since we're not building a high-tech industrial one, the best answer might be a compromise. For the robot's arm we'll use hydraulics, because they are powerful, easy to hook up, and work so much like our own muscles. But later on, when we get to building our robot's body and the systems that will let our robot walk, roll, or creep, we'll use electrics.

The perfect system hasn't been invented yet, especially if you would rather build a humanlike robot instead of an industrial one. But we can guess at what it might be: a synthetic plastic-metal material that would contract as power was applied to it, almost the way our own muscles do. It would work directly without gearing, the way hydraulics do, but without the hoses and pumps, so it would hook up with wires as easily as an electric motor.

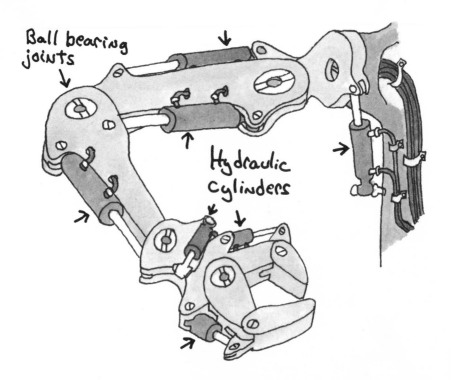

Ball bearing
joints

Hydraulic
cylinders

3/Sense

Our robot arm now has the mechanical systems to move like our own arms move. But it's still just a dumb machine and little more than a high-tech spaghetti tong. It can't move on its own. It needs someone to work its controls to make it move. And it can't feel.

Why should a robot need to feel? It's only metal and can't get hurt.

Think for a minute what it would be like if you didn't have any of your senses. Smell and taste you could probably get along without. Take away sight and hearing and it would be harder, though millions of people get along all right without them. But then take away touch, and you'd really be in trouble.

Suppose you wanted to pick something up. To begin with, you'd have no way of finding it. You could try feeling around for it, but you'd have no way of knowing if you had your hand right on it! If it was red-hot you could burn your hand without ever realizing it. Or if it was too heavy

27

you might rip yourself apart trying to lift it. Without senses our robot would have all these problems.

Our own senses let us avoid all these problems. Not only do they let us know what's going on around us, they keep us in touch with what's happening within our bodies. Our nervous system is always sending signals back to our brain. If something we're lifting is too hot or too heavy, our nerves will signal so to the brain, and we'll know enough to drop it or stop lifting. Other nerves will tell the brain when we've lifted something high enough, so we know to stop even if our eyes are closed.

These messages-back-to-the-brain are called, in robotics talk, *feedback*. Feedback is the one thing that separates automatic machines like player pianos, clockwork toys, and fixed-sequence robots from true robots. Feedback introduces the possibility of letting a machine react to changes rather than just following a fixed program.

Feedback is such an important concept in robotics and computers that the word has come to be used in many other fields. You'll hear advertising people, psychiatrists, and auto mechanics all talking about feedback. Usually what they mean by feedback is listening to the customer, for a change.

Our robot will get its feedback from the electronic sensors that will make up its nervous system. These are little devices on the ends of wires, ranging in size from that of

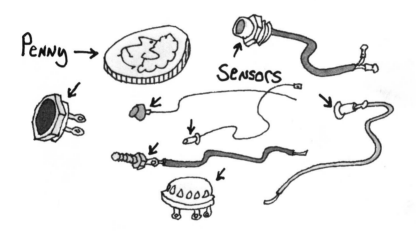

a pea to a pinhead. They measure different inputs depending on what they are made for. Heat, pressure, or light sensors are the most common ones, but others can detect gases, moisture, smoke, or radiation.

We've come to one of the big reasons why it would be very difficult to build a robot that is anywhere as deft, versatile, or sensitive as we are. Our nervous systems have thousands of "sensors" in every inch of our skin, and millions more throughout the insides of our bodies. They supply our brains with an incredible amount of feedback about what's going on inside and outside of us. As a result we can read with our fingertips, detect faint drafts of air, and notice subtle changes of temperature.

Our robot will have to be satisfied with at most a hundred or so sensors. It's not just that the sensors themselves, and

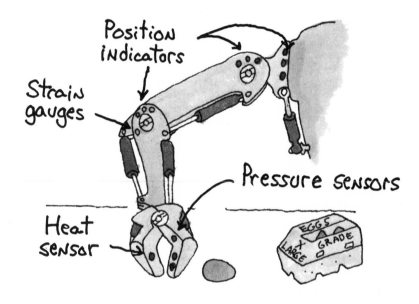

the wiring for them, take up a lot of space. There's a limit to how much feedback our robot's brain can use. Too many sensors will supply it with more feedback than it can handle.

Our robot's hands will be fitted with pressure sensors and temperature sensors so the robot will be able to tell when it's touching something, how hard it's holding on to it, and how hot it is. Other pressure sensors, called *strain gauges*, built into the robot's arm joints will measure the strain there to tell how heavy the objects the robot is lifting are. Other sensors in the arm will just keep track of what position the arm is in.

That takes care of the basic sensors a robot would need. Others could be added depending on any special jobs the robot might have to do. A school-teaching robot would need noise sensors, so it would know when to tell the class to quiet down, and spitball detectors. A fire-fighting robot would need smoke and radiant-heat sensors so it could spot fires from a distance.

How about sight and hearing? It might seem that it would be easy to plug in a television camera or two as eyes and a couple of microphones for ears. But it's not that simple.

We think of ourselves as seeing with our eyes and hearing with our ears. But we really do both with our brain.

Take sight. The eyes just supply signals, like our other nerves do. It's the brain that gives color and shape to things by interpreting these signals.

The problem with using television-camera eyes is that they'd flood the robot's brain with more information than it could handle.

When we see, we also make use of a lifetime of memories and experiences to make sense out of what our eyes are showing us. To fit enough memory into our robot's brain to let it do the same would require a much larger brain than we'll be able to fit in our robot, and a much larger one than it really needs.

Movie Robots

The fifties were years as good for movie robots as they were for rock 'n' roll. Metal people of all sorts lumbered through the sci-fi movies and movie serials, which were shown with the movies to try to hook the audience into coming back the following week.

Most of these film robots were low budget at best. The worst of them looked like not very good Halloween costumes made with cardboard and silver paint. But there were also some very good ones.

Two of the most memorable were Gort, from *The Day the Earth Stood Still*, and Robbie the Robot from *Forbidden Planet*. Gort, a member of a corps of robot peacekeepers who will eventually reduce earth to a cinder if we don't mend our ways, is a good example of the big and clunky school of robot design. But Gort will be remembered where better robots are forgotten for the cryptic command "Klaatu Borada Niktu."

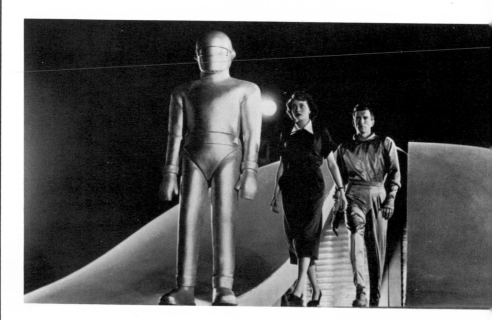

Robbie is an especially fine-looking robot for the times, and was the first cute robot to appear in the movies. Helpful and charming, he plays servant and protector to a mad scientist and his beautiful daughter.

A better system for our robot would be a simple radar or sonar system, which uses sound the way a bat does. This would give the robot the location and shape of objects without flooding it with too much unusable information about them.

SONAR could give position and size of obstacles

That's not to say that no robots use television sight. Some industrial and experimental robots do, but usually only for simple jobs, like sorting objects by color, where the robot can be set to respond to only a few key aspects of what it's seeing.

Hearing doesn't present quite the same problem. Even though our robot will not be smart enough to understand everything it hears, or to talk, it will still be useful for it to be able to hear and respond to noises and simple commands. If we give it two microphones as ears, and mount them a little apart from each other, our robot will be able to locate where a noise is coming from by comparing how loud the noise is in each "ear." Otherwise, our robot wouldn't be able to come when we called!

— Seen from above —

Microphone

← Noise source

1.

Robot (top view) →

Noise is much louder in the left microphone "ear."

Microphone

2.

Robot turns left until noise is equally loud in both ears and is facing the source.

3.

_4/ Thought_____

Now we've come to the most difficult part of building our robot: the brain. Our robot's brain will have a very complicated job. It will have to be able to accept instructions as you tell it what to do, and remember these instructions long enough to carry them out. It will also need to have stored in its memory any other information it will need in order to obey you. And it will need to be able to handle all the feedback from its sensors telling the robot what it is doing and what's going on around it, the way our brain listens to the feedback from the nervous system. Then the robot's brain must be able to make enough sense out of all this information to be able to operate the robot's motors and valves to make it do whatever it's supposed to do!

If it is to do all this, our robot will need a powerful electronic computer for a brain.

But how can a machine do all this? How can a machine think? Actually, a computer doesn't think, at least not in the way you or I do. A computer is basically just a collection of switches. What it does is process information, or *input* as it's called, in order to come up with its conclusions, or *output*. The information that is input and output is called *data*, which is why computers are also referred to as *data processors*.

Here's a simple fire-fighting computer. You feed it information about three danger signs, and it decides how serious the danger is and tells you what to do: One danger sign and it signals low alert; two and it signals high alert; three and the computer commands you to put out the fire. When there are no danger signs at all, the computer says "relax."

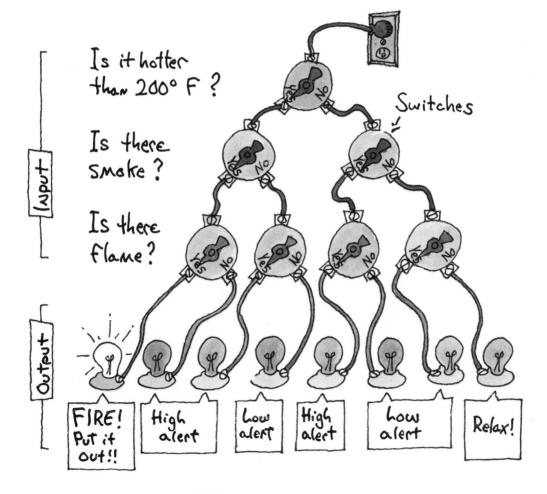

Keep in mind that this is only a computer, not a robot. It can't find out anything, or take any action, by itself. We must give it the information and take the action. All it does is make a decision based on the input we supply. If we give it false information, it'll come to a wrong conclusion.

We feed data into the computer by turning the switches to either the *yes* or the *no* position. There's no middle position on the switches for *maybe* or *I don't know* because computers hate maybes. Since they can't guess or make things up, they must have all the necessary data or they will not work.

You can trace the flow of electricity through the computer by following the wires through, answering each question as you come to it, and seeing where you end up.

No matter what position the switches are in, one of the lights has to light up. It has no choice. That's how any computer works. For a certain set of inputs there can be only one possible logical output. The computer has no choice but to give the right answer, just like our little fire-fighting computer has no choice but to light the right bulb.

If all a computer is is a bunch of switches, then how can it have a memory? Once again, it doesn't, at least not in the way we do. A computer can't daydream. It doesn't have thousands of random thoughts and memories drifting on the fringes of consciousness, almost forgotten, but available for recall if needed, the way we do.

What memory a computer has is created by the arrangement of the switches. Our computer doesn't know a fire from a groundhog, but because of the way we've labeled the input switches and the output lights, it "remembers" that for something to be a fire it must be hot, bright, and smoky, and that if it is a fire it should be put out!

We could, by using special switches called *relays* that can be turned on and off electrically, wire sensors directly to the computer so you wouldn't have to work the yes-no switches. The sensors could then provide their own input directly to the computer. And instead of lights, we could wire the outputs to operate the fire extinguisher itself. Then instead of a simple fire-fighting computer we'd have a fire-fighting robot!

There are a couple of other interesting things about our computer worth noticing. One is that it doesn't have to be electric. You could use chutes instead of wires, and gates

R2D2 and C3PO from *Star Wars*

As the fifties came to a close, Hollywood lost interest in robots and sci-fi, though the Japanese picked up where Hollywood left off and produced a number of forgettable robots.

What few robots did appear in the movies were often as not androids, robots that looked like normal people, and were conveniently played by normal actors and actresses. Dull stuff after Gort and Robbie.

Then, in 1977, with almost no advance hype, a new science-fiction movie appeared out of nowhere to give new life to imaginary robots: George Lucas's *Star Wars*.

Upstaging the film's human stars were two very unlike robots, R2D2 and C3PO. These two robots nicely show two different directions robot evolution might take.

R2D2 is a no-nonsense robot, practical and functional. An only slightly humanoid body houses a powerful computer brain. While R2D2 has two basic limbs and can transport himself about, he usually works as a control unit, connecting himself directly to the equipment he will be operating. He can also hook himself up to other computers for rapid exchange of information.

C3PO, on the other hand, is very humanoid-looking, and almost too human in his fussy behavior. His gorgeous gold plating and his programming in court etiquette make it clear he is meant to be an ornamental toy of the rich, much the way that wealthy people of a hundred or so years ago on our planet would dress their servants in splendid gold-braided uniforms.

instead of switches, then roll marbles down the chutes and still get the same answers.

The other interesting thing is that the same computer can do an entirely different job without our changing the wiring—we just have to change the labels. It could, for example, easily be an adding machine.

As computers go, ours is not a very efficient or powerful one. We could make it more powerful by adding row after row of switches, but since each new input requires twice as many switches as the last, it would quickly become very complicated.

If you're starting to think, "Wait a minute! Computers can't really be all that simple," you're right. Real computers work a little differently than ours. But the basic principle is the same. All the data the computer will work with is reduced to simple *yes* or *no* statements that the computer can process as *electricity on* or *electricity off*.

The "switches" in a real computer are tiny electronic building blocks called *logic gates*. These logic gates are built into little solid-state electronic integrated-circuit chips that look like little gray or black bugs. One I.C. chip can hold so many logic gates that an entire simple computer can be based on one chip, although a powerful computer will use many, many chips.

You'll often hear computer people talking about *programming* computers. All programming means is setting up the computer to do a certain job. When we labeled the inputs and outputs of our fire-fighting computer, we were programming it. When we changed them to make it an adding machine, we reprogrammed it.

Actually, a computer doesn't know whether it's computing the value of pi to the ten millionth place, playing a video game, or running a robot. To make the computer work for us, we have to assign meaning to its input and output, or program it, as we did when we labeled the switches and lights on our computer.

This could be a lot of work with a complicated computer. So rather than having to trace and label all the circuits to program them, real computers are usually designed with built-in programs, called a computer language. This lets us "talk" to them through a keyboard and screen so we can program them quickly.

Even with the keyboard and computer language, programming can be slow, hard work. You can get a good idea why by playing a game with a friend in which you have to tell her every move to make, and she must in turn do exactly that and nothing more. To make it harder, you aren't allowed to combine several moves into one command. Instead of saying, "Walk down the hall to the kitchen," you'll have to say, "Lift your right foot. Move it forward. Put it down. Stop. Now lift your left foot. . . ." It's hard to get anything done quickly that way. Now let's play the same game, only this time you have to type each command on the typewriter. And you have to sit down and write a list all at once that will get your friend through the entire day. It would be pretty hard. Forget one detail and your friend might find herself walking in front of a car, stuck against a wall trying to take two more steps forward, or missing lunch. That's what it can be like programming a robot!

There are ways around this, though. The smarter and more powerful the computer brain in our robot is, the easier programming becomes. That's because the computer can remember earlier programs and incorporate them into new ones so you don't have to repeat yourself. For example, after programming it to walk step by step once, you could just tell the robot to "walk" the next time.

We have several choices of how to program our robot. We could work out its programs on a separate, more powerful computer, then transfer them to the robot's brain. Or we could build in a keyboard and screen.

It would be nice if we could speak to our robot directly, without using a keyboard, but that has its problems. While scientists are working very hard at teaching robots to talk, it is not an easy job. For one thing, human languages are so complicated we probably couldn't fit a big enough computer in our robot to handle even one. And you would

have to be very careful to say exactly what you meant. For example, if you told a robot to "make the bed," it might not know whether to be a maid or a carpenter. Telling it to "rock the baby" or "toss the salad" could be disastrous.

Probably the best compromise would be to go with the built-in keyboard, but to also equip the robot with microphone sound sensors and program the robot's brain to respond to a few phrases that would set in motion programs already stored in its memory. So you could tell it to "Start!" "Walk!" or "Stop!" Or you could say, "Algol, program seven" (assuming that its name is Algol). We could also, without going to all the trouble of giving the robot full powers of speech, equip it with several useful stock replies, such as, "I obey, O Master!" or "At once, puny flesh creature," or "What you ask of me, human, is hardly possible."

There's another programming shortcut, called the *playback method.* Video-game freaks will find themselves right at home with it. After you've spent a few hours (or weeks!) punching out programs for your robot, it might occur to you that it would be a lot easier if you could just show it what to do instead of having to spell out each and every move. That's just how the playback method works, and it's used to program most industrial robots today. A remote control device called a *teaching box* is hooked up to the robot. The teaching box has switches and joysticks on it like the controls for some very complicated video game, and lets you control the robot directly as if it were a big remote-controlled toy. While you're showing the robot what to do, the robot's brain is busy remembering how

46

it's done so the robot will be able to do it by itself next time.

The teaching box is great for teaching the robot basic moves, but isn't much use for more complicated instructions like "guard my bicycle until school is over," so our robot will still need the keyboard and screen.

There just isn't enough room in our robot's computer brain to hold everything the robot may need to know. So some information or complicated directions it doesn't need all the time are stored on disks or magnetic bubbles. The computer, instead of filling its memory with information it may not need, just has to remember where to look if it does need something. It's the same idea as when your parents are going away for a few days, and after giving you routine instructions, they tell you where to look for written instructions and phone numbers for less likely emergencies.

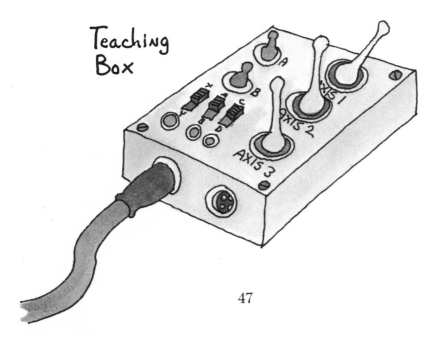

Teaching Box

Robot "Pets"

Robot pets have always been a favorite of home robot builders because the simple life of a dog or cat is much easier to mimic in a robot than our own confused lives.

Some of the earliest and best of the robot pets were the "tortoises" of William Grey Walter, an English scientist. These tiny robots would roam about the house on their own. When they met up with an obstacle they would back up, change course slightly, and go forward again, repeating this until they got around it. When they became hungry as their batteries wore down, they would home in on a light above their recharging station, where they would get an electric "meal."

Not much, compared to C3PO or an industrial robot that can flawlessly weld together an entire car? But it was a robotic milestone. For these machines were the first ever that, once built, could live on their own, making for themselves the moves and decisions necessary for them to go on functioning. And it was done in 1940, without any of the electronics we take for granted today!

The same concept has been taken much further, making full use of the modern computer technology that William Grey Walter didn't have, by Frank DaCosta in his book *How to Build Your Own Working Robot Pet*. His robot can be built in any of several stages, ranging from a simple tortoise-style pet to a state-of-the-art electronic monster that will take over your house if you let it.

Machina Speculatrix

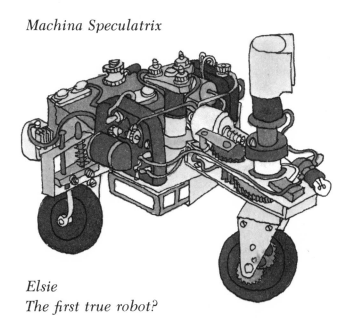

Elsie
The first true robot?

Elsie finding her way around an obstacle.

Tapes or disks can also be used to store programs on, so our robot can be quickly reprogrammed from one job to another without losing the first program.

Computers can do amazing things. They are very fast and can handle huge amounts of data. But they cannot have hunches, daydream, or lie. Programmers have tricks they use to make a computer seem smarter or more human than it really is. We could program our robot's brain so that instead of responding "Yes," it would alternate between "You bet," "Right on," and "Sure," and end every few sentences with "Good buddy" or "Old sport." Anyone communicating with it would be amazed at how natural it sounded, but inside it would be just another unhuman computer following its program, processing bits of data.

When it comes to actually building our robot's brain, we have several choices. We can buy the necessary computer and memory integrated-circuit chips, disk drives, and other electronic bits and pieces, and build it from scratch. Or we can buy a ready-made computer "off the shelf" and adapt it to our robot. Building from scratch is more work, but it lets us match the brain perfectly to our robot's needs.

There's one more important bit of electronic hardware we'll need before we're done. Since the computer brain doesn't speak the same electronic language as the robot's valves, switches, and sensors, it'll need several interfaces. These are electronic translators that link the robot's brain to its muscles and nerves.

One last problem. We may have a hard time fitting all this computer hardware into our robot. The boring but practical solution would be to keep the computer separate,

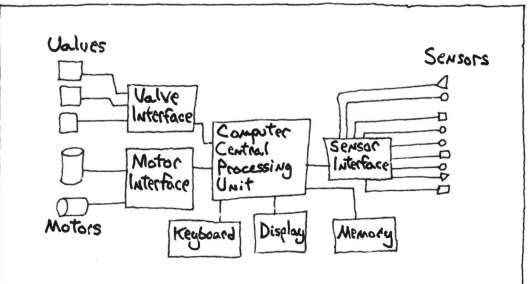

Valves

Valve Interface

Motor Interface

Motors

Computer Central Processing Unit

Keyboard

Display

Sensor Interface

Sensors

Memory

The BRAIN, MUSCLES AND NERVES

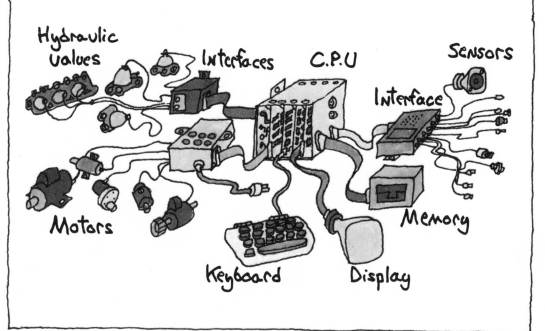

Hydraulic Values

Interfaces

C.P.U

Sensors

Interface

Motors

Memory

Keyboard

Display

and control the robot through a cable or by radio control. If the robot was going to live dangerously, that might not be a bad idea, since the brain is the most expensive part of a robot.

But there's a better way. It doesn't make any difference to the computer how big the robot it's controlling is; just how many motors, valves, and sensors it has. We can just scale up our robot until it's big enough to fit the computer. Or make it even bigger, just for fun. Imagine a four-story-high robot with a control room in its head!

_5/ Putting It All Together__

By now you, the robot builder, have spent much time and money, bought and installed dozens of hydraulic cylinders and motors, wired up handfuls of sensors to a computer brain, and all you've got to show for it is a robot arm.

But to build that arm you had to learn about and make use of all the technologies—mechanical, electric, and electronic (what's the difference? Electric means motors and switches; electronic, computers and radios)—you would need to build the entire robot. You can easily go on designing and building until you have a complete, humanlike robot.

But if the robot was being designed to just weld or handle a tool, it might occur to you to just bolt the arm to the wall and let it go to work and start earning its keep. And that, just about, is what most real-life robot engineers have had to do.

Adding legs, for example, would just about double the number of moving parts the robot would need. Not only

that, but any time you add parts to a machine unnecessarily, you add all sorts of problems down the line you might not think of right away. Cost is the most obvious thing you'd be increasing, but you'd also be doubling the chance of breakdown, and the likely "down time"—the amount of time a machine spends unable to work because it's being serviced or repaired.

Legs are a special challenge, since such delicate control is required to stay balanced while walking upright. We just don't notice it because we've been doing it so long, but watch a year-old baby try to walk! It would take a much more powerful computer brain to handle all the extra parts needed for a robot to walk.

If the robot really needed to get around, some wheels or Caterpillar tracks, like a bulldozer uses, and a simple steering system could do the same job with many fewer parts.

We've come to the reason why robots today don't look much like what we think robots should look like. Robots are expensive machines. In order to pay for themselves they must be as efficient as possible. Robot engineers make them efficient by designing them to be as simple as possible and still adaptable enough to do their jobs well. As a result, most modern robots consist of an arm, often with a tool attached to it, mounted on a swiveling pedestal base. K.I.S.S.!

The computer that does the robot's thinking is usually located separately from the mechanical parts, where it won't get damaged or be in the way, and where the pro-

grammer can get to it easily to reprogram it. Usually the computer will be wired to the computers running the other robots on the same job, or one computer will control many robots. You could argue that, when one computer brain controls many robots, they should all be considered together as making up one vast multiarmed robot!

Fortunately, we're not robot engineers trying to work

Industrial Robots

However much these robots may look like just dull and complicated machines, they are, for now at least, the real thing if you're talking robots. Most of them follow the same pattern as the ones shown, consisting of an arm with movement in several axes on a rotating pedestal.

To really appreciate them you've got to see them at work, and marvel at the uncanny accuracy with which the arm, deftly and precisely, does whatever job it has been programmed to do. In the case of the robot in the lower picture, the job is applying a sealant to the seams of a car body after welding. But it could just as easily, with a change of programming and tools, be doing the welding itself, or cleaning up the welds with a grinding wheel, or painting them.

Both of these are designed to be used in automated factories where all the work is done by robots like them. Factory executives like these robots because they can, once programmed, do the same job over and over again flawlessly. They don't get bored or sick, or have a bad day. And they don't need overtime pay or Social Security.

But other people question the wisdom of industries rushing to automate. What's the point, they ask, when there are so many people needing jobs? And if we replace all the workers with machines, who will buy all the goods the robots flawlessly manufacture? Other robots?

These are good questions. But it doesn't seem to be our nature to question where new technology will lead us ahead of time; instead, we tend to leap in with both feet. If we'd known about pollution, fuel crises, ugly parking lots and freeways, and 50,000 highway deaths a year, would we ever have let the automobile so take over our world?

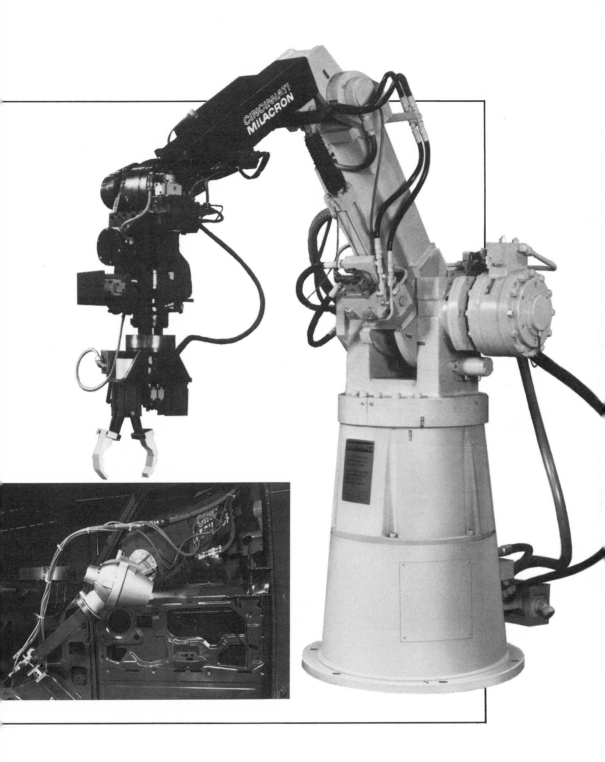

within a tight budget, so we don't have to worry about whether each part is necessary. Since our robot is imaginary, our budget is as well, so we can spend as much as we want to build a humanlike robot!

We'll need another arm, just like the first. We could get fancy and build them differently so our robot can have one agile arm and many-fingered hand for delicate work, and another great big brute claw for rough stuff.

We'll need a body to mount the arms on. It doesn't have to be anything fancy, just a place to hang the arms. Inside it'll be filled with the motors and valves for the hydraulic system, and the electronics for the robot's brain. If we make the body so the shoulders can swivel on ball bearings, the robot will be able to swivel its arms from side to side without having to move its whole body.

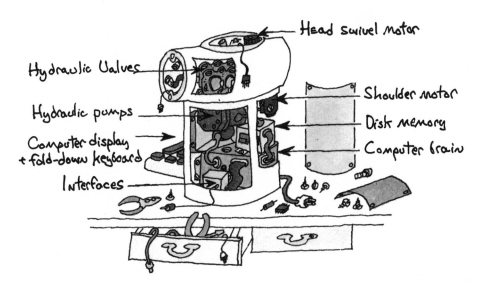

We also need a power source inside the robot's body to run the hydraulic pumps and supply its brain with electricity. This could be almost anything—electric, gas, even steam. It would be nice to use a little nuclear power unit so the robot would almost never need refueling, but the thought of a tiny atomic reactor playing softball with us makes me very nervous! And besides, we couldn't build one small enough to fit. A gas or diesel engine would be easy to fit in, but would pollute too much to use indoors. That leaves electricity. So we'll use electric motors running off batteries so the robot will be self-contained and won't need an extension cord.

To make the robot as self-sufficient as possible, we'll put solar cells all over its body so the sun can recharge the batteries.

Actually, it would take many more solar cells than we can fit on the robot to provide enough power to run it unless we build a very lazy robot that spends all its time sunning itself at the beach. It'll still need an electric plug so it can recharge itself from a wall outlet if it needs to.

We've already talked about why legs are a major problem in building a robot, and why they might not be the most practical way to go (not that we have to be practical!). We've got another problem to deal with now. Batteries, if they are going to store enough power to do any real amount of work, are bulky and heavy, and we are rapidly running out of room inside our robot's body. We could give up trying to make it self-contained and run it off a long extension cord. Or we could kill two birds with one stone and mount our robot on a wheeled or Cat-tracked carriage instead of legs, and use the space inside for batteries. Our robot will look a little less human, and a little more like a mechanical version of a centaur, the horseman of Greek mythology, which is not at all a bad thing to look like.

Since Cat-tracks can tear up a rug pretty quickly, and we will want our robot to be able to come into the house, a good choice would be to use fat all-terrain-vehicle-type rubber tires that can go just about anywhere but won't scratch up good floors.

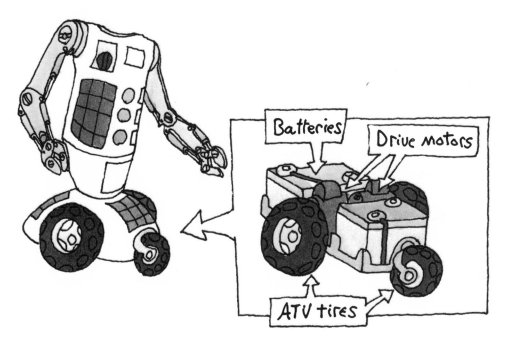

Batteries

Drive motors

ATV tires

STYLING

What a machine looks like is often as much a result of styling as of the mechanical parts underneath. A robot's looks are especially important because they can affect how people will feel towards it.

Take, for example:

The Super-clean Industrial look

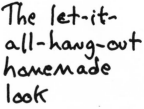

The let-it-all-hang-out homemade look

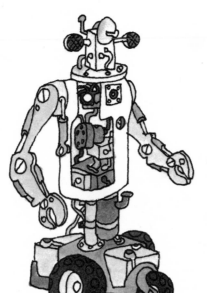

Microphone "ears"

SONAR "eyes"

Nose - just for looks

"Mouth" loudspeaker

To finish off our robot we'll need a head to hold the sonar apparatus, light sensors, microphones, and loud-speaker mouth. Actually, we could just as easily put all of this in the robot's body, but we have heads so why shouldn't our robot? If we mount the head on ball bearings and use a small electric motor, it'll be able to turn independently of the body, which might be useful, and anyway will look neat.

Our robot is finished. All it needs is a name. While it doesn't look overly humanlike, it's a lot closer than most robots today. Best of all, though, is that it's a real robot, able to think, move, and feel for itself, rather than a show-bot that looks better than it performs. And for now, it's as close as we can come using readily available technology. But what's state-of-the-art now will be outdated very soon!

_6/Your Next Robot —————

One thing it's safe to say about robots is that anything you can write about them will already be out of date by the time it's read. That's how fast robot technology is moving ahead.

All over the country and the world, in universities, businesses, and government laboratories, research is underway into building better robots.

Most of this research is aimed at industrial robots. But the improved hardware that comes out of it will be usable in robots of all kinds.

The most spectacular progress in robot development will come in the robot brains, though it's not likely that any totally new kind of computer that better imitates the human mind will be invented. Most experts say computers will go on working the same way they do now, but they'll continue to steadily grow smaller, cheaper, and more powerful.

Your next robot will be much, much smarter than the

Personal Robots

Does building your own robot sound like too much bother? Now you can buy your own personal household robot. Just as computers have trickled out of the offices and universities and into the home, we are now seeing the first generation of home robots. But there's a difference. While the home computers are small in size and price only, and pack the same power that a few years ago would have cost millions and filled several rooms, you'll be in for a disappointment if you expect one of these robots to take over your household chores.

The most sophisticated of them, like the Heath Hero, have a single arm, just like a modern industrial robot, and can be programmed by the owner. But programming it to do a complicated job, like washing the car or weeding the garden, may take more patience and brainpower than either you or the robot is likely to have.

The less sophisticated of these home robots don't even have an arm, and are more computers on wheels than what we think of as robots. Most of them can be programmed to navigate around a room unaided (so they can be equipped with a vacuum cleaning attachment), and have some speech abilities so they can amuse you and your friends.

The manufacturers of these robots would be the first to admit that they are not the all-purpose cooks, maids, and helpers of sci-fi, but are instead intended to be both entertaining "pets" and tools for teaching yourself robotic basics. And anyway, they assure us, these robots are only the first generation, and smarter ones are on their way!

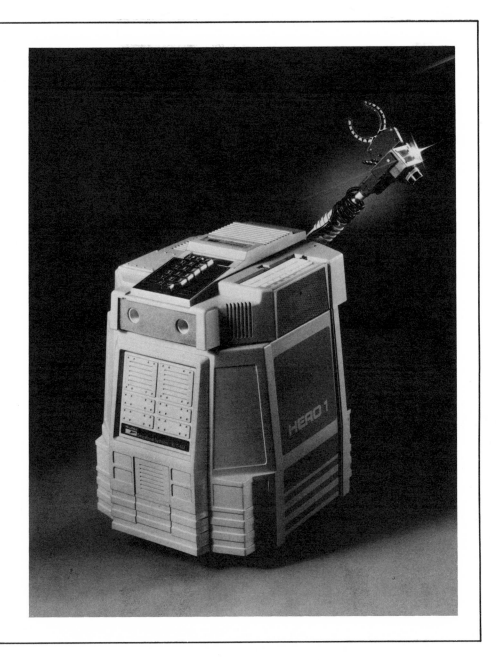

last one. And that's very good news for anyone trying to build a humanlike robot.

A lot of the things we would have liked our robot to have, like robot speech or legged walking systems, exist already, but only in the laboratory. The problem is that, as of now, they require more computer power to operate than we could ever fit into our robot.

With tomorrow's smarter computers it will be a different story. Full speech and partial sight will be possible. Programming your next robot could be as simple as talking to a friend.

Another area where we can expect a lot of progress is in the robot's senses, since a robot's usefulness is directly related to how deftly it can feel and sense.

Plastic skin with many built-in sensors to the square inch will let your next robot feel the shape of whatever it's holding. It'll also let the robot pick up anything, from an egg to a heavy motor part, without risk of crushing or dropping it.

Mechanical systems will go on improving more slowly. We're not likely to see any amazing breakthroughs there, because the basic mechanical systems have been around for a long time, and engineers are pretty familiar with what can and can't be done.

If you were not satisfied with the wheels on our robot, your next one will be able to walk, but not necessarily on two legs. Researchers working on walking robots are trying various numbers of legs, with six being a favorite!

One thing we can't expect in the near future is that the price of robots will plunge as spectacularly as computer

prices have over the last few years. Why not? Robots have just too many mechanical parts, and there are no shortcuts to making a machine. Computers can be made cheaper by figuring out ways to make the parts smaller and squeezing more computing power into each tiny part. Once a new electronic part is designed, it is cheap to manufacture, and the costs of labor and materials to make the parts are so small as to hardly matter.

But no matter how cheaply and efficiently you can make a machine, the metals and plastics and labor that go into it are still expensive enough to keep the price up.

Still, a household robot wouldn't have to be made as ruggedly as an industrial one, since it wouldn't be working 24 hours a day or handling such heavy jobs. And since the cost of its computer brain makes up a large share of the price of a robot, we can expect to see somewhat cheaper home robots someday, made in automated factories by other robots!

Will we ever see "real" robots outside of TV and the movie theater? Walking, thinking, and talking robots like Gort or C3PO? Probably. However expensive and impractical such robots might be now for everyday work, they hold a strong fascination for all of us. As robot technology progresses, the showbots will become more and more like working robots until the showbots become useful machines instead of gimmicks. But even an occasional handmade one-of-a-kind showpiece is a long way from the race of helpful and obedient metal servants that science fiction has promised us for so long.

Eventually, though, there'll come a time when robot components will become so cheap and widely available that, instead of building special tools to fit the robot to each job, we'll be able to build robots that can use the same tools we do. That way one robot can do many jobs without having to be modified for each new task—just like us. Then maybe we'll see humanlike robots, interchangeable, for some things at least, with people themselves.

Whether or not this will be a good idea only time will tell.

Index _____